North of Boston

*By Robert
Frost*

TO

E. M. F.
THIS BOOK OF
PEOPLE

Table of Contents

The Pasture

I'M going out to clean the pasture spring;
I'll only stop to rake the leaves away
(And wait to watch the water clear, I may):
I sha'n't be gone long.—You come too.
I'm going out to fetch the little calf
That's standing by the mother. It's so young,
It totters when she licks it with her tongue.
I sha'n't be gone long.—You come too.

Mending Wall

SOMETHING there is that doesn't love a wall,
That sends the frozen-ground-swell under it,
And spills the upper boulders in the sun;

And makes gaps even two can pass abreast.

The work of hunters is another thing:

I have come after them and made repair

Where they have left not one stone on a stone,

But they would have the rabbit out of hiding,

To please the yelping dogs. The gaps I mean,

No one has seen them made or heard them made,

But at spring mending-time we find them there.

I let my neighbour know beyond the hill;

And on a day we meet to walk the line

And set the wall between us once again.

We keep the wall between us as we go.

To each the boulders that have fallen to each.

And some are loaves and some so nearly balls

We have to use a spell to make them balance:

"Stay where you are until our backs are turned!"

We wear our fingers rough with handling them.

Oh, just another kind of out-door
game,
One on a side. It comes to little more:
There where it is we do not need the
wall:
He is all pine and I am apple orchard.
My apple trees will never get across
And eat the cones under his pines, I
tell him.
He only says, "Good fences make
good neighbours."
Spring is the mischief in me, and I
wonder
If I could put a notion in his head:
"Why do they make good neighbours?
Isn't it
Where there are cows? But here there
are no cows.
Before I built a wall I'd ask to know
What I was walling in or walling out,
And to whom I was like to give
offence.
Something there is that doesn't love a
wall,
That wants it down." I could say
"Elves" to him,
But it's not elves exactly, and I'd rather
He said it for himself. I see him there
Bringing a stone grasped firmly by the
top
In each hand, like an old-stone savage
armed.

He moves in darkness as it seems to me,

Not of woods only and the shade of trees.

He will not go behind his father's saying,

And he likes having thought of it so well

He says again, "Good fences make good neighbours."

The Death of the
Hired Man

MARY sat musing on the lamp-flame at the table

Waiting for Warren. When she heard his step,

She ran on tip-toe down the darkened passage

To meet him in the doorway with the news

And put him on his guard. "Silas is back."

She pushed him outward with her through the door

And shut it after her. "Be kind," she said.

She took the market things from
Warren's arms

And set them on the porch, then drew
him down

To sit beside her on the wooden steps.

"When was I ever anything but kind to
him?

But I'll not have the fellow back," he
said.

"I told him so last haying, didn't I?

'If he left then,' I said, 'that ended it.'

What good is he? Who else will
harbour him

At his age for the little he can do?

What help he is there's no depending
on.

Off he goes always when I need him
most.

'He thinks he ought to earn a little pay,

Enough at least to buy tobacco with,

So he won't have to beg and be
beholden.'

'All right,' I say, 'I can't afford to pay

Any fixed wages, though I wish I
could.'

'Someone else can.' 'Then someone
else will have to.'

I shouldn't mind his bettering himself

If that was what it was. You can be
certain,

When he begins like that, there's
someone at him

Trying to coax him off with pocket-money,—

In haying time, when any help is scarce.

In winter he comes back to us. I'm done."

"Sh! not so loud: he'll hear you," Mary said.

"I want him to: he'll have to soon or late."

"He's worn out. He's asleep beside the stove.

When I came up from Rowe's I found him here,

Huddled against the barn-door fast asleep,

A miserable sight, and frightening, too—

You needn't smile—I didn't recognise him—

I wasn't looking for him—and he's changed.

Wait till you see."

"Where did you say he'd been?"

"He didn't say. I dragged him to the house,

And gave him tea and tried to make him smoke.

I tried to make him talk about his travels.

Nothing would do: he just kept nodding off."

"What did he say? Did he say
anything?"

"But little."

"Anything? Mary, confess

He said he'd come to ditch the
meadow for me."

"Warren!"

"But did he? I just want to know."

"Of course he did. What would you
have him say?

Surely you wouldn't grudge the poor
old man

Some humble way to save his self-
respect.

He added, if you really care to know,

He meant to clear the upper pasture,
too.

That sounds like something you have
heard before?

Warren, I wish you could have heard
the way

He jumbled everything. I stopped to
look

Two or three times—he made me feel
so queer—

To see if he was talking in his sleep.

He ran on Harold Wilson—you
remember—

The boy you had in haying four years
since.

He's finished school, and teaching in
his college.

Silas declares you'll have to get him back.

He says they two will make a team for work:

Between them they will lay this farm as smooth!

The way he mixed that in with other things.

He thinks young Wilson a likely lad, though daft

On education—you know how they fought

All through July under the blazing sun,

Silas up on the cart to build the load,

Harold along beside to pitch it on."

"Yes, I took care to keep well out of earshot."

"Well, those days trouble Silas like a dream.

You wouldn't think they would. How some things linger!

Harold's young college boy's assurance piqued him.

After so many years he still keeps finding

Good arguments he sees he might have used.

I sympathise. I know just how it feels

To think of the right thing to say too late.

Harold's associated in his mind with Latin.

He asked me what I thought of Harold's saying

He studied Latin like the violin

Because he liked it—that an argument!

He said he couldn't make the boy believe

He could find water with a hazel prong—

Which showed how much good school had ever done him.

He wanted to go over that. But most of all

He thinks if he could have another chance

To teach him how to build a load of hay——"

"I know, that's Silas' one accomplishment.

He bundles every forkful in its place,

And tags and numbers it for future reference,

So he can find and easily dislodge it

In the unloading. Silas does that well.

He takes it out in bunches like big birds' nests.

You never see him standing on the hay

He's trying to lift, straining to lift himself."

"He thinks if he could teach him that, he'd be

Some good perhaps to someone in the world.

He hates to see a boy the fool of books.

Poor Silas, so concerned for other folk,

And nothing to look backward to with pride,

And nothing to look forward to with hope,

So now and never any different."

Part of a moon was falling down the west,

Dragging the whole sky with it to the hills.

Its light poured softly in her lap. She saw

And spread her apron to it. She put out her hand

Among the harp-like morning-glory strings,

Taut with the dew from garden bed to eaves,

As if she played unheard the tenderness

That wrought on him beside her in the night.

"Warren," she said, "he has come home to die:

You needn't be afraid he'll leave you
this time."

"Home," he mocked gently.

"Yes, what else but home?
It all depends on what you mean by
home.
Of course he's nothing to us, any more
Than was the hound that came a
stranger to us
Out of the woods, worn out upon the
trail."

"Home is the place where, when you
have to go there,
They have to take you in."

"I should have called it
Something you somehow haven't to
deserve."

Warren leaned out and took a step or
two,
Picked up a little stick, and brought it
back
And broke it in his hand and tossed it
by.

"Silas has better claim on us you think
Than on his brother? Thirteen little
miles
As the road winds would bring him to
his door.
Silas has walked that far no doubt to-
day.
Why didn't he go there? His brother's
rich,

A somebody—director in the bank."

"He never told us that."

"We know it though."

"I think his brother ought to help, of
course.

I'll see to that if there is need. He
ought of right

To take him in, and might be willing
to—

He may be better than appearances.

But have some pity on Silas. Do you
think

If he'd had any pride in claiming kin

Or anything he looked for from his
brother,

He'd keep so still about him all this
time?"

"I wonder what's between them."

"I can tell you.

Silas is what he is—we wouldn't mind
him—

But just the kind that kinsfolk can't
abide.

He never did a thing so very bad.

He don't know why he isn't quite as
good

As anyone. He won't be made
ashamed

To please his brother, worthless
though he is."

"I can't think Si ever hurt anyone."

"No, but he hurt my heart the way he lay

And rolled his old head on that sharp-edged chair-back.

He wouldn't let me put him on the lounge.

You must go in and see what you can do.

I made the bed up for him there to-night.

You'll be surprised at him—how much he's broken.

His working days are done; I'm sure of it."

"I'd not be in a hurry to say that."

"I haven't been. Go, look, see for yourself.

But, Warren, please remember how it is:

He's come to help you ditch the meadow.

He has a plan. You mustn't laugh at him.

He may not speak of it, and then he may.

I'll sit and see if that small sailing cloud

Will hit or miss the moon."

It hit the moon.

Then there were three there, making a dim row,

The moon, the little silver cloud, and
she.
Warren returned—too soon, it seemed
to her,
Slipped to her side, caught up her
hand and waited.
"Warren," she questioned.
"Dead," was all he answered.

The Mountain

THE mountain held the town as in a
shadow
I saw so much before I slept there
once:
I noticed that I missed stars in the
west,
Where its black body cut into the sky.
Near me it seemed: I felt it like a wall
Behind which I was sheltered from a
wind.
And yet between the town and it I
found,
When I walked forth at dawn to see
new things,
Were fields, a river, and beyond, more
fields.
The river at the time was fallen away,

And made a widespread brawl on
cobble-stones;
But the signs showed what it had done
in spring;
Good grass-land gullied out, and in the
grass
Ridges of sand, and driftwood stripped
of bark.
I crossed the river and swung round
the mountain.
And there I met a man who moved so
slow
With white-faced oxen in a heavy cart,
It seemed no hand to stop him
altogether.
"What town is this?" I asked.
"This? Lunenburg."
Then I was wrong: the town of my
sojourn,
Beyond the bridge, was not that of the
mountain,
But only felt at night its shadowy
presence.
"Where is your village? Very far from
here?"
"There is no village—only scattered
farms.
We were but sixty voters last election.
We can't in nature grow to many
more:
That thing takes all the room!" He
moved his goad.

The mountain stood there to be
pointed at.
Pasture ran up the side a little way,
And then there was a wall of trees
with trunks:
After that only tops of trees, and cliffs
Imperfectly concealed among the
leaves.
A dry ravine emerged from under
boughs
Into the pasture.
"That looks like a path.
Is that the way to reach the top from
here?—
Not for this morning, but some other
time:
I must be getting back to breakfast
now."
"I don't advise your trying from this
side.
There is no proper path, but those that
have
Been up, I understand, have climbed
from Ladd's.
That's five miles back. You can't
mistake the place:
They logged it there last winter some
way up.
I'd take you, but I'm bound the other
way."
"You've never climbed it?"
"I've been on the sides

Deer-hunting   and   trout-fishing.
There's a brook
That starts up on it somewhere—I've
heard say
Right on the top, tip-top—a curious
thing.
But what would interest you about the
brook,
It's always cold in summer, warm in
winter.
One of the great sights going is to see
It steam in winter like an ox's breath,
Until the bushes all along its banks
Are inch-deep with the frosty spines
and bristles—
You know the kind. Then let the sun
shine on it!"
"There ought to be a view around the
world
From such a mountain—if it isn't
wooded
Clear to the top." I saw through leafy
screens
Great granite terraces in sun and
shadow,
Shelves one could rest a knee on
getting up—
With depths behind him sheer a
hundred feet;
Or turn and sit on and look out and
down,

With little ferns in crevices at his elbow.

"As to that I can't say. But there's the spring,

Right on the summit, almost like a fountain.

That ought to be worth seeing."

"If it's there.

You never saw it?"

"I guess there's no doubt

About its being there. I never saw it.

It may not be right on the very top:

It wouldn't have to be a long way down

To have some head of water from above,

And a good distance down might not be noticed

By anyone who'd come a long way up.

One time I asked a fellow climbing it

To look and tell me later how it was."

"What did he say?"

"He said there was a lake

Somewhere in Ireland on a mountain top."

"But a lake's different. What about the spring?"

"He never got up high enough to see.

That's why I don't advise your trying this side.

He tried this side. I've always meant to go

And look myself, but you know how it
is:
It doesn't seem so much to climb a
mountain
You've worked around the foot of all
your life.
What would I do? Go in my overalls,
With a big stick, the same as when the
cows
Haven't come down to the bars at
milking time?
Or with a shotgun for a stray black
bear?
'Twouldn't seem real to climb for
climbing it."
"I shouldn't climb it if I didn't want
to—
Not for the sake of climbing. What's
its name?"
"We call it Hor: I don't know if that's
right."
"Can one walk around it? Would it be
too far?"
"You can drive round and keep in
Lunenburg,
But it's as much as ever you can do,
The boundary lines keep in so close to
it.
Hor is the township, and the
township's Hor—
And a few houses sprinkled round the
foot,

Like boulders broken off the upper cliff,

Rolled out a little farther than the rest."

"Warm in December, cold in June, you say?"

"I don't suppose the water's changed at all.

You and I know enough to know it's warm

Compared with cold, and cold compared with warm.

But all the fun's in how you say a thing."

"You've lived here all your life?"

"Ever since Hor

Was no bigger than a——" What, I did not hear.

He drew the oxen toward him with light touches

Of his slim goad on nose and offside flank,

Gave them their marching orders and was moving.

A Hundred
Collars

LANCASTER bore him—such a little town,
Such a great man. It doesn't see him often
Of late years, though he keeps the old homestead
And sends the children down there with their mother
To run wild in the summer—a little wild.
Sometimes he joins them for a day or two
And sees old friends he somehow can't get near.
They meet him in the general store at night,
  Pre-occupied with formidable mail,
  Rifling a printed letter as he talks.
They seem afraid. He wouldn't have it so:
  Though a great scholar, he's a democrat,
  If not at heart, at least on principle.
  Lately when coming up to Lancaster
  His train being late he missed another train
  And had four hours to wait at Woodsville Junction
  After eleven o'clock at night. Too tired
  To think of sitting such an ordeal out,
  He turned to the hotel to find a bed.

"No room," the night clerk said.
"Unless———"

Woodsville's a place of shrieks and
wandering lamps

And cars that shook and rattle—and
one hotel.

"You say 'unless.'"

"Unless you wouldn't mind
Sharing a room with someone else."

"Who is it?"

"A man."

"So I should hope. What kind of
man?"

"I know him: he's all right. A man's a
man.

Separate beds of course you
understand."

The night clerk blinked his eyes and
dared him on.

"Who's that man sleeping in the office
chair?

Has he had the refusal of my chance?"

"He was afraid of being robbed or
murdered.

What do you say?"

"I'll have to have a bed."

The night clerk led him up three
flights of stairs

And down a narrow passage full of
doors,

At the last one of which he knocked
and entered.

"Lafe, here's a fellow wants to share your room."

"Show him this way. I'm not afraid of him.

I'm not so drunk I can't take care of myself."

The night clerk clapped a bedstead on the foot.

"This will be yours. Good-night," he said, and went.

"Lafe was the name, I think?"

"Yes, Layfayette.

You got it the first time. And yours?"

"Magoon.

Doctor Magoon."

"A Doctor?"

"Well, a teacher."

"Professor   Square-the-circle-till-you're-tired?

Hold on, there's something I don't think of now

That I had on my mind to ask the first

Man that knew anything I happened in with.

I'll ask you later—don't let me forget it."

The Doctor looked at Lafe and looked away.

A man? A brute. Naked above the waist,

He sat there creased and shining in the light,

Fumbling the buttons in a well-
starched shirt.

"I'm moving into a size-larger shirt.

I've felt mean lately; mean's no name
for it.

I just found what the matter was to-
night:

I've been a-choking like a nursery tree

When it outgrows the wire band of its
name tag.

I blamed it on the hot spell we've been
having.

'Twas nothing but my foolish hanging
back,

Not liking to own up I'd grown a size.

Number eighteen this is. What size do
you wear?"

The Doctor caught his throat
convulsively.

"Oh—ah—fourteen—fourteen."

"Fourteen! You say so!

I can remember when I wore fourteen.

And come to think I must have back at
home

More than a hundred collars, size
fourteen.

Too bad to waste them all. You ought
to have them.

They're yours and welcome; let me
send them to you.

What makes you stand there on one
leg like that?

You're not much furtherer than where Kike left you.

You act as if you wished you hadn't come.

Sit down or lie down, friend; you make me nervous."

The Doctor made a subdued dash for it,

And propped himself at bay against a pillow.

"Not that way, with your shoes on Kike's white bed.

You can't rest that way. Let me pull your shoes off."

"Don't touch me, please—I say, don't touch me, please.

I'll not be put to bed by you, my man."

"Just as you say. Have it your own way then.

'My man' is it? You talk like a professor.

Speaking of who's afraid of who, however,

I'm thinking I have more to lose than you

If anything should happen to be wrong.

Who wants to cut your number fourteen throat!

Let's have a show down as an evidence

Of good faith. There is ninety dollars.

Come, if you're not afraid."

"I'm not afraid.

There's five: that's all I carry."

"I can search you?

Where are you moving over to? Stay still.

You'd better tuck your money under you

And sleep on it the way I always do

When I'm with people I don't trust at night."

"Will you believe me if I put it there

Right on the counterpane—that I do trust you?"

"You'd say so, Mister Man.—I'm a collector.

My ninety isn't mine—you won't think that.

I pick it up a dollar at a time

All round the country for the Weekly News,

Published in Bow. You know the Weekly News?"

"Known it since I was young."

"Then you know me.

Now we are getting on together— talking.

I'm sort of Something for it at the front.

My business is to find what people want:

They pay for it, and so they ought to
have it.

Fairbanks, he says to me—he's
editor—

Feel out the public sentiment—he
says.

A good deal comes on me when all is
said.

The only trouble is we disagree

In politics: I'm Vermont Democrat—

You know what that is, sort of double-
dyed;

The News has always been
Republican.

Fairbanks, he says to me, 'Help us this
year,'

Meaning by us their ticket. 'No,' I
says,

'I can't and won't. You've been in long
enough:

It's time you turned around and
boosted us.

You'll have to pay me more than ten a
week

If I'm expected to elect Bill Taft.

I doubt if I could do it anyway.'"

"You seem to shape the paper's
policy."

"You see I'm in with everybody, know
'em all.

I almost know their farms as well as
they do."

"You drive around? It must be pleasant work."

"It's business, but I can't say it's not fun.

What I like best's the lay of different farms,

Coming out on them from a stretch of woods,

Or over a hill or round a sudden corner.

I like to find folks getting out in spring,

Raking the dooryard, working near the house.

Later they get out further in the fields.

Everything's shut sometimes except the barn;

The family's all away in some back meadow.

There's a hay load a-coming—when it comes.

And later still they all get driven in:

The fields are stripped to lawn, the garden patches

Stripped to bare ground, the apple trees

To whips and poles. There's nobody about.

The chimney, though, keeps up a good brisk smoking.

And I lie back and ride. I take the reins

Only when someone's coming, and the mare

Stops when she likes: I tell her when to go.

I've spoiled Jemima in more ways than one.

She's got so she turns in at every house

As if she had some sort of curvature,

No matter if I have no errand there.

She thinks I'm sociable. I maybe am.

It's seldom I get down except for meals, though.

Folks entertain me from the kitchen doorstep,

All in a family row down to the youngest."

"One would suppose they might not be as glad

To see you as you are to see them."

"Oh,

Because I want their dollar. I don't want

Anything they've not got. I never dun.

I'm there, and they can pay me if they like.

I go nowhere on purpose: I happen by.

Sorry there is no cup to give you a drink.

I drink out of the bottle—not your style.

Mayn't I offer you——?"

"No, no, no, thank you."

"Just as you say. Here's looking at you then.—

And now I'm leaving you a little while.

You'll rest easier when I'm gone, perhaps—

Lie down—let yourself go and get some sleep.

But first—let's see—what was I going to ask you?

Those collars—who shall I address them to,

Suppose you aren't awake when I come back?"

"Really, friend, I can't let you. You— may need them."

"Not till I shrink, when they'll be out of style."

"But really I—I have so many collars."

"I don't know who I rather would have have them.

They're only turning yellow where they are.

But you're the doctor as the saying is.

I'll put the light out. Don't you wait for me:

I've just begun the night. You get some sleep.

I'll knock so-fashion and peep round the door

When I come back so you'll know who
it is.

There's nothing I'm afraid of like
scared people.

I don't want you should shoot me in
the head.

What am I doing carrying off this
bottle?

There now, you get some sleep."

He shut the door.

The Doctor slid a little down the
pillow.

Home Burial

HE saw her from the bottom of the
stairs

Before she saw him. She was starting
down,

Looking back over her shoulder at
some fear.

She took a doubtful step and then
undid it

To raise herself and look again. He
spoke

Advancing toward her: "What is it you
see

From up there always—for I want to
know."

She turned and sank upon her skirts at that,

And her face changed from terrified to dull.

He said to gain time: "What is it you see,"

Mounting until she cowered under him.

"I will find out now—you must tell me, dear."

She, in her place, refused him any help

With the least stiffening of her neck and silence.

She let him look, sure that he wouldn't see,

Blind creature; and a while he didn't see.

But at last he murmured, "Oh," and again, "Oh."

"What is it—what?" she said.

"Just that I see."

"You don't," she challenged. "Tell me what it is."

"The wonder is I didn't see at once.

I never noticed it from here before.

I must be wonted to it—that's the reason.

The little graveyard where my people are!

So small the window frames the whole of it.

Not so much larger than a bedroom, is
it?

There are three stones of slate and one
of marble,

Broad-shouldered little slabs there in
the sunlight

On the sidehill. We haven't to mind
those.

But I understand: it is not the stones,

But the child's mound———"

"Don't, don't, don't, don't," she cried.

She withdrew shrinking from beneath
his arm

That rested on the banister, and slid
downstairs;

And turned on him with such a
daunting look,

He said twice over before he knew
himself:

"Can't a man speak of his own child
he's lost?"

"Not you! Oh, where's my hat? Oh, I
don't need it!

I must get out of here. I must get air.

I don't know rightly whether any man
can."

"Amy! Don't go to someone else this
time.

Listen to me. I won't come down the
stairs."

He sat and fixed his chin between his
fists.

"There's something I should like to ask
you, dear."

"You don't know how to ask it."

"Help me, then."

Her fingers moved the latch for all
reply.

"My words are nearly always an
offence.

I don't know how to speak of anything

So as to please you. But I might be
taught

I should suppose. I can't say I see how.

A man must partly give up being a
man

With women-folk. We could have
some arrangement

By which I'd bind myself to keep
hands off

Anything special you're a-mind to
name.

Though I don't like such things 'twixt
those that love.

Two that don't love can't live together
without them.

But two that do can't live together with
them."

She moved the latch a little. "Don't—
don't go.

Don't carry it to someone else this
time.

Tell me about it if it's something
human.

Let me into your grief. I'm not so much

Unlike other folks as your standing there

Apart would make me out. Give me my chance.

I do think, though, you overdo it a little.

What was it brought you up to think it the thing

To take your mother-loss of a first child

So inconsolably—in the face of love.

You'd think his memory might be satisfied——"

"There you go sneering now!"

"I'm not, I'm not!

You make me angry. I'll come down to you.

God, what a woman! And it's come to this,

A man can't speak of his own child that's dead."

"You can't because you don't know how.

If you had any feelings, you that dug

With your own hand—how could you?—his little grave;

I saw you from that very window there,

Making the gravel leap and leap in air,

Leap up, like that, like that, and land
so lightly

And roll back down the mound beside
the hole.

I thought, Who is that man? I didn't
know you.

And I crept down the stairs and up the
stairs

To look again, and still your spade
kept lifting.

Then you came in. I heard your
rumbling voice

Out in the kitchen, and I don't know
why,

But I went near to see with my own
eyes.

You could sit there with the stains on
your shoes

Of the fresh earth from your own
baby's grave

And talk about your everyday
concerns.

You had stood the spade up against
the wall

Outside there in the entry, for I saw
it."

"I shall laugh the worst laugh I ever
laughed.

I'm cursed. God, if I don't believe I'm
cursed."

"I can repeat the very words you were
saying.

'Three foggy mornings and one rainy day

Will rot the best birch fence a man can build.'

Think of it, talk like that at such a time!

What had how long it takes a birch to rot

To do with what was in the darkened parlour.

You couldn't care! The nearest friends can go

With anyone to death, comes so far short

They might as well not try to go at all.

No, from the time when one is sick to death,

One is alone, and he dies more alone.

Friends make pretence of following to the grave,

But before one is in it, their minds are turned

And making the best of their way back to life

And living people, and things they understand.

But the world's evil. I won't have grief so

If I can change it. Oh, I won't, I won't!"

"There, you have said it all and you feel better.

You won't go now. You're crying.
Close the door.
The heart's gone out of it: why keep it
up.
Amy! There's someone coming down
the road!"
"You—oh, you think the talk is all. I
must go—
Somewhere out of this house. How
can I make you——"
"If—you—do!" She was opening the
door wider.
"Where do you mean to go? First tell
me that.
I'll follow and bring you back by
force. I will!—"

The Black
Cottage

WE chanced in passing by that
afternoon
To catch it in a sort of special picture
Among tar-banded ancient cherry
trees,
Set well back from the road in rank
lodged grass,
The little cottage we were speaking of,

A front with just a door between two windows,

Fresh painted by the shower a velvet black.

We paused, the minister and I, to look.

He made as if to hold it at arm's length

Or put the leaves aside that framed it in.

"Pretty," he said. "Come in. No one will care."

The path was a vague parting in the grass

That led us to a weathered window-sill.

We pressed our faces to the pane. "You see," he said,

"Everything's as she left it when she died.

Her sons won't sell the house or the things in it.

They say they mean to come and summer here

Where they were boys. They haven't come this year.

They live so far away—one is out west—

It will be hard for them to keep their word.

Anyway they won't have the place disturbed."

A buttoned hair-cloth lounge spread scrolling arms

Under a crayon portrait on the wall
Done   sadly   from   an   old
daguerreotype.
"That was the father as he went to war.
She always, when she talked about
war,
Sooner or later came and leaned, half
knelt
Against the lounge beside it, though I
doubt
If such unlifelike lines kept power to
stir
Anything in her after all the years.
He   fell   at   Gettysburg   or
Fredericksburg,
I   ought   to   know—it   makes   a
difference which:
Fredericksburg wasn't Gettysburg, of
course.
But what I'm getting to is how
forsaken
A   little   cottage   this   has   always
seemed;
Since she went more than ever, but
before—
I don't mean altogether by the lives
That had gone out of it, the father first,
Then the two sons, till she was left
alone.
(Nothing could draw her after those
two sons.
She valued the considerate neglect

She had at some cost taught them after years.)

I mean by the world's having passed it by—

As we almost got by this afternoon.

It always seems to me a sort of mark

To measure how far fifty years have brought us.

Why not sit down if you are in no haste?

These doorsteps seldom have a visitor.

The warping boards pull out their own old nails

With none to tread and put them in their place.

She had her own idea of things, the old lady.

And she liked talk. She had seen Garrison

And Whittier, and had her story of them.

One wasn't long in learning that she thought

Whatever else the Civil War was for

It wasn't just to keep the States together,

Nor just to free the slaves, though it did both.

She wouldn't have believed those ends enough

To have given outright for them all she gave.

Her giving somehow touched the principle

That all men are created free and equal.

And to hear her quaint phrases—so removed

From the world's view to-day of all those things.

That's a hard mystery of Jefferson's.

What did he mean? Of course the easy way

Is to decide it simply isn't true.

It may not be. I heard a fellow say so.

But never mind, the Welshman got it planted

Where it will trouble us a thousand years.

Each age will have to reconsider it.

You couldn't tell her what the West was saying,

And what the South to her serene belief.

She had some art of hearing and yet not

Hearing the latter wisdom of the world.

White was the only race she ever knew.

Black she had scarcely seen, and yellow never.

But how could they be made so very unlike

By the same hand working in the same
stuff?

She had supposed the war decided
that.

What are you going to do with such a
person?

Strange how such innocence gets its
own way.

I shouldn't be surprised if in this world

It were the force that would at last
prevail.

Do you know but for her there was a
time

When to please younger members of
the church,

Or rather say non-members in the
church,

Whom we all have to think of
nowadays,

I would have changed the Creed a
very little?

Not that she ever had to ask me not to;

It never got so far as that; but the bare
thought

Of her old tremulous bonnet in the
pew,

And of her half asleep was too much
for me.

Why, I might wake her up and startle
her.

It was the words 'descended into
Hades'

That seemed too pagan to our liberal
youth.

You know they suffered from a
general onslaught.

And well, if they weren't true why
keep right on

Saying them like the heathen? We
could drop them.

Only—there was the bonnet in the
pew.

Such a phrase couldn't have meant
much to her.

But suppose she had missed it from
the Creed

As a child misses the unsaid Good-
night,

And falls asleep with heartache—how
should I feel?

I'm just as glad she made me keep
hands off,

For, dear me, why abandon a belief

Merely because it ceases to be true.

Cling to it long enough, and not a
doubt

It will turn true again, for so it goes.

Most of the change we think we see in
life

Is due to truths being in and out of
favour.

As I sit here, and oftentimes, I wish

I could be monarch of a desert land

I could devote and dedicate forever

To the truths we keep coming back
and back to.

So desert it would have to be, so
walled

By mountain ranges half in summer
snow,

No one would covet it or think it
worth

The pains of conquering to force
change on.

Scattered oases where men dwelt, but
mostly

Sand dunes held loosely in tamarisk

Blown over and over themselves in
idleness.

Sand grains should sugar in the natal
dew

The babe born to the desert, the sand
storm

Retard   mid-waste   my   cowering
caravans—

"There are bees in this wall." He
struck the clapboards,

Fierce heads looked out; small bodies
pivoted.

We rose to go. Sunset blazed on the
windows.

Blueberries

"YOU ought to have seen what I saw
on my way

To the village, through Mortenson's
pasture to-day:

Blueberries as big as the end of your
thumb,

Real sky-blue, and heavy, and ready to
drum

In the cavernous pail of the first one to
come!

And all ripe together, not some of
them green

And some of them ripe! You ought to
have seen!"

"I don't know what part of the pasture
you mean."

"You know where they cut off the
woods—let me see—

It was two years ago—or no!—can it
be

No longer than that?—and the
following fall

The fire ran and burned it all up but
the wall."

"Why, there hasn't been time for the
bushes to grow.

That's always the way with the
blueberries, though:

There may not have been the ghost of
a sign

Of them anywhere under the shade of
the pine,

But get the pine out of the way, you may burn

The pasture all over until not a fern

Or grass-blade is left, not to mention a stick,

And presto, they're up all around you as thick

And hard to explain as a conjuror's trick."

"It must be on charcoal they fatten their fruit.

I taste in them sometimes the flavour of soot.

And after all really they're ebony skinned:

The blue's but a mist from the breath of the wind,

A tarnish that goes at a touch of the hand,

And less than the tan with which pickers are tanned."

"Does Mortenson know what he has, do you think?"

"He may and not care and so leave the chewink

To gather them for him—you know what he is.

He won't make the fact that they're rightfully his

An excuse for keeping us other folk out."

"I wonder you didn't see Loren about."

"The best of it was that I did. Do you know,

I was just getting through what the field had to show

And over the wall and into the road,

When who should come by, with a democrat-load

Of all the young chattering Lorens alive,

But Loren, the fatherly, out for a drive."

"He saw you, then? What did he do? Did he frown?"

"He just kept nodding his head up and down.

You know how politely he always goes by.

But he thought a big thought—I could tell by his eye—

Which being expressed, might be this in effect:

'I have left those there berries, I shrewdly suspect,

To ripen too long. I am greatly to blame.'"

"He's a thriftier person than some I could name."

"He seems to be thrifty; and hasn't he need,

With the mouths of all those young Lorens to feed?

He has brought them all up on wild
berries, they say,
Like birds. They store a great many
away.
They eat them the year round, and
those they don't eat
They sell in the store and buy shoes
for their feet."
"Who cares what they say? It's a nice
way to live,
Just taking what Nature is willing to
give,
Not forcing her hand with harrow and
plow."
"I wish you had seen his perpetual
bow—
And the air of the youngsters! Not one
of them turned,
And they looked so solemn-absurdly
concerned."
"I wish I knew half what the flock of
them know
Of where all the berries and other
things grow,
Cranberries in bogs and raspberries on
top
Of the boulder-strewn mountain, and
when they will crop.
I met them one day and each had a
flower
Stuck into his berries as fresh as a
shower;

Some strange kind—they told me it
hadn't a name."

"I've told you how once not long after
we came,

I almost provoked poor Loren to mirth
By going to him of all people on earth
To ask if he knew any fruit to be had

For the picking. The rascal, he said
he'd be glad

To tell if he knew. But the year had
been bad.

There had been some berries—but
those were all gone.

He didn't say where they had been. He
went on:

'I'm sure—I'm sure'—as polite as
could be.

He spoke to his wife in the door, 'Let
me see,

Mame, we don't know any good
berrying place?'

It was all he could do to keep a
straight face.

"If he thinks all the fruit that grows
wild is for him,

He'll find he's mistaken. See here, for
a whim,

We'll pick in the Mortensons' pasture
this year.

We'll go in the morning, that is, if it's
clear,

And the sun shines out warm: the vines must be wet.

It's so long since I picked I almost forget

How we used to pick berries: we took one look round,

Then sank out of sight like trolls underground,

And saw nothing more of each other, or heard,

Unless when you said I was keeping a bird

Away from its nest, and I said it was you.

'Well, one of us is.' For complaining it flew

Around and around us. And then for a while

We picked, till I feared you had wandered a mile,

And I thought I had lost you. I lifted a shout

Too loud for the distance you were, it turned out,

For when you made answer, your voice was as low

As talking—you stood up beside me, you know."

"We sha'n't have the place to ourselves to enjoy—

Not likely, when all the young Lorens deploy.

They'll be there to-morrow, or even to-
night.

They won't be too friendly—they may
be polite—

To people they look on as having no
right

To pick where they're picking. But we
won't complain.

You ought to have seen how it looked
in the rain,

The fruit mixed with water in layers of
leaves,

Like two kinds of jewels, a vision for
thieves."

A Servant to
Servants

I DIDN'T make you know how glad I
was

To have you come and camp here on
our land.

I promised myself to get down some
day

And see the way you lived, but I don't
know!

With a houseful of hungry men to feed

I guess you'd find.... It seems to me

I can't express my feelings any more

Than I can raise my voice or want to lift

My hand (oh, I can lift it when I have to).

Did ever you feel so? I hope you never.

It's got so I don't even know for sure

Whether I am glad, sorry, or anything.

There's nothing but a voice-like left inside

That seems to tell me how I ought to feel,

And would feel if I wasn't all gone wrong.

You take the lake. I look and look at it.

I see it's a fair, pretty sheet of water.

I stand and make myself repeat out loud

The advantages it has, so long and narrow,

Like a deep piece of some old running river

Cut short off at both ends. It lies five miles

Straight away through the mountain notch

From the sink window where I wash the plates,

And all our storms come up toward the house,

Drawing the slow waves whiter and whiter and whiter.

It took my mind off doughnuts and soda biscuit

To step outdoors and take the water dazzle

A sunny morning, or take the rising wind

About my face and body and through my wrapper,

When a storm threatened from the Dragon's Den,

And a cold chill shivered across the lake.

I see it's a fair, pretty sheet of water,

Our Willoughby! How did you hear of it?

I expect, though, everyone's heard of it.

In a book about ferns? Listen to that!

You let things more like feathers regulate

Your going and coming. And you like it here?

I can see how you might. But I don't know!

It would be different if more people came,

For then there would be business. As it is,

The cottages Len built, sometimes we rent them,

Sometimes we don't. We've a good piece of shore

That ought to be worth something, and may yet.

But I don't count on it as much as Len.

He looks on the bright side of everything,

Including me. He thinks I'll be all right

With doctoring. But it's not medicine—

Lowe is the only doctor's dared to say so—

It's rest I want—there, I have said it out—

From cooking meals for hungry hired men

And washing dishes after them—from doing

Things over and over that just won't stay done.

By good rights I ought not to have so much

Put on me, but there seems no other way.

Len says one steady pull more ought to do it.

He says the best way out is always through.

And I agree to that, or in so far

As that I can see no way out but through—

Leastways for me—and then they'll be
convinced.

It's not that Len don't want the best for
me.

It was his plan our moving over in

Beside the lake from where that day I
showed you

We used to live—ten miles from
anywhere.

We didn't change without some
sacrifice,

But Len went at it to make up the loss.

His work's a man's, of course, from
sun to sun,

But he works when he works as hard
as I do—

Though there's small profit in
comparisons.

(Women and men will make them all
the same.)

But work ain't all. Len undertakes too
much.

He's into everything in town. This year

It's highways, and he's got too many
men

Around him to look after that make
waste.

They take advantage of him
shamefully,

And proud, too, of themselves for
doing so.

We have four here to board, great good-for-nothings,

Sprawling about the kitchen with their talk

While I fry their bacon. Much they care!

No more put out in what they do or say

Than if I wasn't in the room at all.

Coming and going all the time, they are:

I don't learn what their names are, let alone

Their characters, or whether they are safe

To have inside the house with doors unlocked.

I'm not afraid of them, though, if they're not

Afraid of me. There's two can play at that.

I have my fancies: it runs in the family.

My father's brother wasn't right. They kept him

Locked up for years back there at the old farm.

I've been away once—yes, I've been away.

The State Asylum. I was prejudiced;

I wouldn't have sent anyone of mine there;

You know the old idea—the only asylum
Was the poorhouse, and those who could afford,
Rather than send their folks to such a place,
Kept them at home; and it does seem more human.
But it's not so: the place is the asylum.
There they have every means proper to do with,
And you aren't darkening other people's lives—
Worse than no good to them, and they no good
To you in your condition; you can't know
Affection or the want of it in that state.
I've heard too much of the old-fashioned way.
My father's brother, he went mad quite young.
Some thought he had been bitten by a dog,
Because his violence took on the form
Of carrying his pillow in his teeth;
But it's more likely he was crossed in love,
Or so the story goes. It was some girl.
Anyway all he talked about was love.
They soon saw he would do someone a mischief

If he wa'n't kept strict watch of, and it ended
In father's building him a sort of cage,
Or room within a room, of hickory poles,
Like stanchions in the barn, from floor to ceiling,—
A narrow passage all the way around.
Anything they put in for furniture
He'd tear to pieces, even a bed to lie on.
So they made the place comfortable with straw,
Like a beast's stall, to ease their consciences.
Of course they had to feed him without dishes.
They tried to keep him clothed, but he paraded
With his clothes on his arm—all of his clothes.
Cruel—it sounds. I 'spose they did the best
They knew. And just when he was at the height,
Father and mother married, and mother came,
A bride, to help take care of such a creature,
And accommodate her young life to his.

That was what marrying father meant
to her.

She had to lie and hear love things
made dreadful

By his shouts in the night. He'd shout
and shout

Until the strength was shouted out of
him,

And his voice died down slowly from
exhaustion.

He'd pull his bars apart like bow and
bow-string,

And let them go and make them twang
until

His hands had worn them smooth as
any ox-bow.

And then he'd crow as if he thought
that child's play—

The only fun he had. I've heard them
say, though,

They found a way to put a stop to it.

He was before my time—I never saw
him;

But the pen stayed exactly as it was
There in the upper chamber in the ell,
A sort of catch-all full of attic clutter.

I often think of the smooth hickory
bars.

It got so I would say—you know, half
fooling—

"It's time I took my turn upstairs in
jail"—

Just as you will till it becomes a habit.

No wonder I was glad to get away.

Mind you, I waited till Len said the word.

I didn't want the blame if things went wrong.

I was glad though, no end, when we moved out,

And I looked to be happy, and I was,

As I said, for a while—but I don't know!

Somehow the change wore out like a prescription.

And there's more to it than just window-views

And living by a lake. I'm past such help—

Unless Len took the notion, which he won't,

And I won't ask him—it's not sure enough.

I 'spose I've got to go the road I'm going:

Other folks have to, and why shouldn't I?

I almost think if I could do like you,

Drop everything and live out on the ground—

But it might be, come night, I shouldn't like it,

Or a long rain. I should soon get enough,

And be glad of a good roof overhead.

I've lain awake thinking of you, I'll warrant,

More than you have yourself, some of these nights.

The wonder was the tents weren't snatched away

From over you as you lay in your beds.

I haven't courage for a risk like that.

Bless you, of course, you're keeping me from work,

But the thing of it is, I need to be kept.

There's work enough to do—there's always that;

But behind's behind. The worst that you can do

Is set me back a little more behind.

I sha'n't catch up in this world, anyway.

I'd rather you'd not go unless you must.

After Apple-picking

MY long two-pointed ladder's sticking through a tree

Toward heaven still,

And there's a barrel that I didn't fill
Beside it, and there may be two or three
Apples I didn't pick upon some bough.
But I am done with apple-picking now.
Essence of winter sleep is on the night,
The scent of apples: I am drowsing off.
I cannot rub the strangeness from my sight
I got from looking through a pane of glass
I skimmed this morning from the drinking trough
And held against the world of hoary grass.
It melted, and I let it fall and break.
But I was well
Upon my way to sleep before it fell,
And I could tell
What form my dreaming was about to take.
Magnified apples appear and disappear,
Stem end and blossom end,
And every fleck of russet showing clear.
My instep arch not only keeps the ache,

It keeps the pressure of a ladder-round.

I feel the ladder sway as the boughs bend.

And I keep hearing from the cellar bin
The rumbling sound
Of load on load of apples coming in.
For I have had too much
Of apple-picking: I am overtired
Of the great harvest I myself desired.
There were ten thousand thousand fruit to touch,
Cherish in hand, lift down, and not let fall.
For all
That struck the earth,
No matter if not bruised or spiked with stubble,
Went surely to the cider-apple heap
As of no worth.
One can see what will trouble
This sleep of mine, whatever sleep it is.
Were he not gone,
The woodchuck could say whether it's like his
Long sleep, as I describe its coming on,
Or just some human sleep.

The Code

THERE were three in the meadow by
the brook
Gathering up windrows, piling cocks
of hay,
With an eye always lifted toward the
west
Where an irregular sun-bordered cloud
Darkly advanced with a perpetual
dagger
Flickering across its bosom. Suddenly
One helper, thrusting pitchfork in the
ground,
Marched himself off the field and
home. One stayed.
The town-bred farmer failed to
understand.
"What is there wrong?"
"Something you just now said."
"What did I say?"
"About our taking pains."
"To cock the hay?—because it's going
to shower?
I said that more than half an hour ago.
I said it to myself as much as you."
"You didn't know. But James is one
big fool.
He thought you meant to find fault
with his work.
That's what the average farmer would
have meant.

James would take time, of course, to
chew it over
Before he acted: he's just got round to
act."
"He is a fool if that's the way he takes
me."
"Don't let it bother you. You've found
out something.
The hand that knows his business
won't be told
To do work better or faster—those
two things.
I'm as particular as anyone:
Most likely I'd have served you just
the same.
But I know you don't understand our
ways.
You were just talking what was in
your mind,
What was in all our minds, and you
weren't hinting.
Tell you a story of what happened
once:
I was up here in Salem at a man's
Named Sanders with a gang of four or
five
Doing the haying. No one liked the
boss.
He was one of the kind sports call a
spider,
All wiry arms and legs that spread out
wavy

From a humped body nigh as big's a biscuit.

But work! that man could work, especially
If by so doing he could get more work
Out of his hired help. I'm not denying
He was hard on himself. I couldn't find
That he kept any hours—not for himself.
Daylight and lantern-light were one to him:
I've heard him pounding in the barn all night.
But what he liked was someone to encourage.
Them that he couldn't lead he'd get behind
And drive, the way you can, you know, in mowing—
Keep at their heels and threaten to mow their legs off.
I'd seen about enough of his bulling tricks
(We call that bulling). I'd been watching him.
So when he paired off with me in the hayfield
To load the load, thinks I, Look out for trouble.
I built the load and topped it off; old Sanders

Combed it down with a rake and says,
'O. K.'

Everything went well till we reached
the barn

With a big catch to empty in a bay.

You understand that meant the easy
job

For the man up on top of throwing
down

The hay and rolling it off wholesale,

Where on a mow it would have been
slow lifting.

You wouldn't think a fellow'd need
much urging

Under these circumstances, would you
now?

But the old fool seizes his fork in both
hands,

And looking up bewhiskered out of
the pit,

Shouts like an army captain, 'Let her
come!'

Thinks I, D'ye mean it? 'What was that
you said?'

I asked out loud, so's there'd be no
mistake,

'Did you say, Let her come?' 'Yes, let
her come.'

He said it over, but he said it softer.

Never you say a thing like that to a
man,

Not if he values what he is. God, I'd as soon
Murdered him as left out his middle name.
I'd built the load and knew right where to find it.
Two or three forkfuls I picked lightly round for
Like meditating, and then I just dug in
And dumped the rackful on him in ten lots.
I looked over the side once in the dust
And caught sight of him treading-water-like,
Keeping his head above. 'Damn ye,' I says,
'That gets ye!' He squeaked like a squeezed rat.
That was the last I saw or heard of him.
I cleaned the rack and drove out to cool off.
As I sat mopping hayseed from my neck,
And sort of waiting to be asked about it,
One of the boys sings out, 'Where's the old man?'
'I left him in the barn under the hay.
If ye want him, ye can go and dig him out.'

They realized from the way I swobbed my neck

More than was needed something must be up.

They headed for the barn; I stayed where I was.

They told me afterward. First they forked hay,

A lot of it, out into the barn floor.

Nothing! They listened for him. Not a rustle.

I guess they thought I'd spiked him in the temple

Before I buried him, or I couldn't have managed.

They excavated more. 'Go keep his wife

Out of the barn.' Someone looked in a window,

And curse me if he wasn't in the kitchen

Slumped way down in a chair, with both his feet

Stuck in the oven, the hottest day that summer.

He looked so clean disgusted from behind

There was no one that dared to stir him up,

Or let him know that he was being looked at.

Apparently I hadn't buried him

(I may have knocked him down); but
my just trying
To bury him had hurt his dignity.
He had gone to the house so's not to
meet me.
He kept away from us all afternoon.
We tended to his hay. We saw him out
After a while picking peas in his
garden:
He couldn't keep away from doing
something."
"Weren't you relieved to find he wasn't
dead?"
"No! and yet I don't know—it's hard to
say.
I went about to kill him fair enough."
"You took an awkward way. Did he
discharge you?"
"Discharge me? No! He knew I did
just right."

The Generations
of Men

A GOVERNOR it was proclaimed this
time,
When all who would come seeking in
New Hampshire

Ancestral memories might come together.

And those of the name Stark gathered in Bow,

A rock-strewn town where farming has fallen off,

And sprout-lands flourish where the axe has gone.

Someone had literally run to earth

In an old cellar hole in a by-road

The origin of all the family there.

Thence they were sprung, so numerous a tribe

That now not all the houses left in town

Made shift to shelter them without the help

Of here and there a tent in grove and orchard.

They were at Bow, but that was not enough:

Nothing would do but they must fix a day

To stand together on the crater's verge

That turned them on the world, and try to fathom

The past and get some strangeness out of it.

But rain spoiled all. The day began uncertain,

With clouds low trailing and moments of rain that misted.

The young folk held some hope out to each other
Till well toward noon when the storm settled down
With a swish in the grass. "What if the others
Are there," they said. "It isn't going to rain."
Only one from a farm not far away
Strolled thither, not expecting he would find
Anyone else, but out of idleness.
One, and one other, yes, for there were two.
The second round the curving hillside road
Was a girl; and she halted some way off
To reconnoitre, and then made up her mind
At least to pass by and see who he was,
And perhaps hear some word about the weather.
This was some Stark she didn't know. He nodded.
"No fête to-day," he said.
"It looks that way."
She swept the heavens, turning on her heel.
"I only idled down."
"I idled down."

Provision there had been for just such
meeting
Of stranger cousins, in a family tree
Drawn on a sort of passport with the
branch
Of the one bearing it done in detail—
Some zealous one's laborious device.
She made a sudden movement toward
her bodice,
As one who clasps her heart. They
laughed together.
"Stark?" he inquired. "No matter for
the proof."
"Yes, Stark. And you?"
"I'm Stark." He drew his passport.
"You know we might not be and still
be cousins:
The town is full of Chases, Lowes,
and Baileys,
All   claiming   some   priority   in
Starkness.
My mother was a Lane, yet might
have married
Anyone upon earth and still her
children
Would   have   been   Starks,   and
doubtless here to-day."
"You riddle with your genealogy
Like a Viola. I don't follow you."
"I only mean my mother was a Stark
Several times over, and by marrying
father

No more than brought us back into the name."

"One ought not to be thrown into confusion

By a plain statement of relationship,

But I own what you say makes my head spin.

You take my card—you seem so good at such things—

And see if you can reckon our cousinship.

Why not take seats here on the cellar wall

And dangle feet among the raspberry vines?"

"Under the shelter of the family tree."

"Just so—that ought to be enough protection."

"Not from the rain. I think it's going to rain."

"It's raining."

"No, it's misting; let's be fair.

Does the rain seem to you to cool the eyes?"

The situation was like this: the road

Bowed outward on the mountain half-way up,

And disappeared and ended not far off.

No one went home that way. The only house

Beyond where they were was a shattered seedpod.

And below roared a brook hidden in trees,

The sound of which was silence for the place.

This he sat listening to till she gave judgment.

"On father's side, it seems, we're—let me see——"

"Don't be too technical.—You have three cards."

"Four cards, one yours, three mine, one for each branch

Of the Stark family I'm a member of."

"D'you know a person so related to herself

Is supposed to be mad."

"I may be mad."

"You look so, sitting out here in the rain

Studying genealogy with me

You never saw before. What will we come to

With all this pride of ancestry, we Yankees?

I think we're all mad. Tell me why we're here

Drawn into town about this cellar hole

Like wild geese on a lake before a storm?

What do we see in such a hole, I
wonder."
"The Indians had a myth of
Chicamoztoc,
Which means The Seven Caves that
We Came out of.
This is the pit from which we Starks
were digged."
"You must be learned. That's what you
see in it?"
"And what do you see?"
"Yes, what do I see?
First let me look. I see raspberry
vines——"
"Oh, if you're going to use your eyes,
just hear
What I see. It's a little, little boy,
As pale and dim as a match flame in
the sun;
He's groping in the cellar after jam,
He thinks it's dark and it's flooded
with daylight."
"He's nothing. Listen. When I lean like
this
I can make out old Grandsir Stark
distinctly,—
With his pipe in his mouth and his
brown jug—
Bless you, it isn't Grandsir Stark, it's
Granny,
But the pipe's there and smoking and
the jug.

She's after cider, the old girl, she's
thirsty;
    Here's hoping she gets her drink and
gets out safely."
    "Tell me about her. Does she look like
me?"
    "She should, shouldn't she, you're so
many times
    Over descended from her. I believe
    She does look like you. Stay the way
you are.
    The nose is just the same, and so's the
chin—
    Making   allowance,   making   due
allowance."
    "You poor, dear, great, great, great,
great Granny!"
    "See that you get her greatness right.
Don't stint her."
    "Yes, it's important, though you think
it isn't.
    I won't be teased. But see how wet I
am."
    "Yes, you must go; we can't stay here
for ever.
    But wait until I give you a hand up.
    A bead of silver water more or less
    Strung on your hair won't hurt your
summer looks.
    I wanted to try something with the
noise

That the brook raises in the empty
valley.

We have seen visions—now consult
the voices.

Something I must have learned riding
in trains

When I was young. I used the roar

To set the voices speaking out of it,

Speaking or singing, and the band-
music playing.

Perhaps you have the art of what I
mean.

I've never listened in among the
sounds

That a brook makes in such a wild
descent.

It ought to give a purer oracle."

"It's as you throw a picture on a
screen:

The meaning of it all is out of you;

The voices give you what you wish to
hear."

"Strangely, it's anything they wish to
give."

"Then I don't know. It must be strange
enough.

I wonder if it's not your make-believe.

What do you think you're like to hear
to-day?"

"From the sense of our having been
together—

But why take time for what I'm like to
hear?

I'll tell you what the voices really say.

You will do very well right where you
are

A little longer. I mustn't feel too
hurried,

Or I can't give myself to hear the
voices."

"Is this some trance you are
withdrawing into?"

"You must be very still; you mustn't
talk."

"I'll hardly breathe."

"The voices seem to say——"

"I'm waiting."

"Don't! The voices seem to say:

Call her Nausicaa, the unafraid

Of an acquaintance made
adventurously."

"I let you say that—on consideration."

"I don't see very well how you can
help it.

You want the truth. I speak but by the
voices.

You see they know I haven't had your
name,

Though what a name should matter
between us——"

"I shall suspect——"

"Be good. The voices say:

Call her Nausicaa, and take a timber

That you shall find lies in the cellar charred

Among the raspberries, and hew and shape it

For a door-sill or other corner piece

In a new cottage on the ancient spot.

The life is not yet all gone out of it.

And come and make your summer dwelling here,

And perhaps she will come, still unafraid,

And sit before you in the open door

With flowers in her lap until they fade,

But not come in across the sacred sill——"

"I wonder where your oracle is tending.

You can see that there's something wrong with it,

Or it would speak in dialect. Whose voice

Does it purport to speak in? Not old Grandsir's

Nor Granny's, surely. Call up one of them.

They have best right to be heard in this place."

"You seem so partial to our great-grandmother

(Nine times removed. Correct me if I err.)

You will be likely to regard as sacred

Anything she may say. But let me warn you,

Folks in her day were given to plain speaking.

You think you'd best tempt her at such a time?"

"It rests with us always to cut her off."

"Well then, it's Granny speaking: 'I dunnow!

Mebbe I'm wrong to take it as I do.

There ain't no names quite like the old ones though,

Nor never will be to my way of thinking.

One mustn't bear too hard on the new comers,

But there's a dite too many of them for comfort.

I should feel easier if I could see

More of the salt wherewith they're to be salted.

Son, you do as you're told! You take the timber—

It's as sound as the day when it was cut—

And begin over——' There, she'd better stop.

You can see what is troubling Granny, though.

But don't you think we sometimes make too much

Of the old stock? What counts is the ideals,

And those will bear some keeping still about."

"I can see we are going to be good friends."

"I like your 'going to be.' You said just now

It's going to rain."

"I know, and it was raining.

I let you say all that. But I must go now."

"You let me say it? on consideration?

How shall we say good-bye in such a case?"

"How shall we?"

"Will you leave the way to me?"

"No, I don't trust your eyes. You've said enough.

Now give me your hand up.—Pick me that flower."

"Where shall we meet again?"

"Nowhere but here

Once more before we meet elsewhere."

"In rain?"

"It ought to be in rain. Sometime in rain.

In rain to-morrow, shall we, if it rains?

But if we must, in sunshine." So she went.

The
Housekeeper

I LET myself in at the kitchen door.

"It's you," she said. "I can't get up.
Forgive me

Not answering your knock. I can no
more

Let people in than I can keep them
out.

I'm getting too old for my size, I tell
them.

My fingers are about all I've the use of

So's to take any comfort. I can sew:

I help out with this beadwork what I
can."

"That's a smart pair of pumps you're
beading there.

Who are they for?"

"You mean?—oh, for some miss.

I can't keep track of other people's
daughters.

Lord, if I were to dream of everyone

Whose shoes I primped to dance in!"

"And where's John?"

"Haven't you seen him? Strange what
set you off

To come to his house when he's gone
to yours.

You can't have passed each other. I
know what:

He must have changed his mind and
gone to Garlands.

He won't be long in that case. You can
wait.

Though what good you can be, or
anyone—

It's gone so far. You've heard?
Estelle's run off."

"Yes, what's it all about? When did
she go?"

"Two weeks since."

"She's in earnest, it appears."

"I'm sure she won't come back. She's
hiding somewhere.

I don't know where myself. John
thinks I do.

He thinks I only have to say the word,

And she'll come back. But, bless you,
I'm her mother—

I can't talk to her, and, Lord, if I
could!"

"It will go hard with John. What will
he do?

He can't find anyone to take her
place."

"Oh, if you ask me that, what will he
do?

He gets some sort of bakeshop meals
together,
    With me to sit and tell him everything,
    What's wanted and how much and
where it is.
    But when I'm gone—of course I can't
stay here:
    Estelle's to take me when she's settled
down.
    He and I only hinder one another.
    I tell them they can't get me through
the door, though:
    I've been built in here like a big
church organ.
    We've been here fifteen years."
    "That's a long time
    To live together and then pull apart.
    How do you see him living when
you're gone?
    Two of you out will leave an empty
house."
    "I don't just see him living many
years,
    Left here with nothing but the
furniture.
    I hate to think of the old place when
we're gone,
    With the brook going by below the
yard,
    And no one here but hens blowing
about.

If he could sell the place, but then, he can't:
No one will ever live on it again.
It's too run down. This is the last of it.
What I think he will do, is let things smash.
He'll sort of swear the time away. He's awful!
I never saw a man let family troubles
Make so much difference in his man's affairs.
He's just dropped everything. He's like a child.
I blame his being brought up by his mother.
He's got hay down that's been rained on three times.
He hoed a little yesterday for me:
I thought the growing things would do him good.
Something went wrong. I saw him throw the hoe
Sky-high with both hands. I can see it now—
Come here—I'll show you—in that apple tree.
That's no way for a man to do at his age:
He's fifty-five, you know, if he's a day."
"Aren't you afraid of him? What's that gun for?"

"Oh, that's been there for hawks since chicken-time.

John Hall touch me! Not if he knows his friends.

I'll say that for him, John's no threatener

Like some men folk. No one's afraid of him;

All is, he's made up his mind not to stand

What he has got to stand."

"Where is Estelle?

Couldn't one talk to her? What does she say?

You say you don't know where she is."

"Nor want to!

She thinks if it was bad to live with him,

It must be right to leave him."

"Which is wrong!"

"Yes, but he should have married her."

"I know."

"The strain's been too much for her all these years:

I can't explain it any other way.

It's different with a man, at least with John:

He knows he's kinder than the run of men.

Better than married ought to be as good

As married—that's what he has always said.

I know the way he's felt—but all the same!"

"I wonder why he doesn't marry her
And end it."

"Too late now: she wouldn't have him.

He's given her time to think of something else.

That's his mistake. The dear knows my interest

Has been to keep the thing from breaking up.

This is a good home: I don't ask for better.

But when I've said, 'Why shouldn't they be married,'

He'd say, 'Why should they?' no more words than that."

"And after all why should they? John's been fair

I take it. What was his was always hers.

There was no quarrel about property."

"Reason enough, there was no property.

A friend or two as good as own the farm,

Such as it is. It isn't worth the mortgage."

"I mean Estelle has always held the purse."

"The rights of that are harder to get at.

I guess Estelle and I have filled the purse.

'Twas we let him have money, not he us.

John's a bad farmer. I'm not blaming him.

Take it year in, year out, he doesn't make much.

We came here for a home for me, you know,

Estelle to do the housework for the board

Of both of us. But look how it turns out:

She seems to have the housework, and besides,

Half of the outdoor work, though as for that,

He'd say she does it more because she likes it.

You see our pretty things are all outdoors.

Our hens and cows and pigs are always better

Than folks like us have any business with.

Farmers around twice as well off as we

Haven't as good. They don't go with the farm.

One thing you can't help liking about John,

He's fond of nice things—too fond, some would say.

But Estelle don't complain: she's like him there.

She wants our hens to be the best there are.

You never saw this room before a show,

Full of lank, shivery, half-drowned birds

In separate coops, having their plumage done.

The smell of the wet feathers in the heat!

You spoke of John's not being safe to stay with.

You don't know what a gentle lot we are:

We wouldn't hurt a hen! You ought to see us

Moving a flock of hens from place to place.

We're not allowed to take them upside down,

All we can hold together by the legs.

Two at a time's the rule, one on each arm,

No matter how far and how many times

We have to go."

"You mean that's John's idea."

"And we live up to it; or I don't know
What childishness he wouldn't give
way to.

He manages to keep the upper hand
On his own farm. He's boss. But as to
hens:

We fence our flowers in and the hens
range.

Nothing's too good for them. We say it
pays.

John likes to tell the offers he has had,
Twenty for this cock, twenty-five for
that.

He never takes the money. If they're
worth

That much to sell, they're worth as
much to keep.

Bless you, it's all expense, though.
Reach me down

The little tin box on the cupboard
shelf,

The upper shelf, the tin box. That's the
one.

I'll show you. Here you are."

"What's this?"

"A bill—

For fifty dollars for one Langshang
cock—

Receipted. And the cock is in the
yard."

"Not in a glass case, then?"

"He'd need a tall one:

He can eat off a barrel from the ground.

He's been in a glass case, as you may say,

The Crystal Palace, London. He's imported.

John bought him, and we paid the bill with beads—

Wampum, I call it. Mind, we don't complain.

But you see, don't you, we take care of him."

"And like it, too. It makes it all the worse."

"It seems as if. And that's not all: he's helpless

In ways that I can hardly tell you of.

Sometimes he gets possessed to keep accounts

To see where all the money goes so fast.

You know how men will be ridiculous.

But it's just fun the way he gets bedeviled—

If he's untidy now, what will he be— —?

"It makes it all the worse. You must be blind."

"Estelle's the one. You needn't talk to me."

"Can't you and I get to the root of it?

What's the real trouble? What will satisfy her?"

"It's as I say: she's turned from him, that's all."

"But why, when she's well off? Is it the neighbours,

Being cut off from friends?"

"We have our friends.

That isn't it. Folks aren't afraid of us."

"She's let it worry her. You stood the strain,

And you're her mother."

"But I didn't always.

I didn't relish it along at first.

But I got wonted to it. And besides—

John said I was too old to have grandchildren.

But what's the use of talking when it's done?

She won't come back—it's worse than that—she can't."

"Why do you speak like that? What do you know?

What do you mean?—she's done harm to herself?"

"I mean she's married—married someone else."

"Oho, oho!"

"You don't believe me."

"Yes, I do,

Only too well. I knew there must be
something!

So that was what was back. She's bad,
that's all!"

"Bad to get married when she had the
chance?"

"Nonsense! See what's she done! But
who, who——"

"Who'd marry her straight out of such
a mess?

Say it right out—no matter for her
mother.

The man was found. I'd better name
no names.

John himself won't imagine who he
is."

"Then it's all up. I think I'll get away.

You'll be expecting John. I pity
Estelle;

I suppose she deserves some pity, too.

You ought to have the kitchen to
yourself

To break it to him. You may have the
job."

"You needn't think you're going to get
away.

John's almost here. I've had my eye on
someone

Coming down Ryan's Hill. I thought
'twas him.

Here he is now. This box! Put it away.
And this bill."

"What's the hurry? He'll unhitch."

"No, he won't, either. He'll just drop
the reins

And turn Doll out to pasture, rig and
all.

She won't get far before the wheels
hang up

On something—there's no harm. See,
there he is!

My, but he looks as if he must have
heard!"

John threw the door wide but he didn't
enter.

"How are you, neighbour? Just the
man I'm after.

Isn't it Hell," he said. "I want to know.

Come out here if you want to hear me
talk.

I'll talk to you, old woman, afterward.

I've got some news that maybe isn't
news.

What are they trying to do to me, these
two?"

"Do go along with him and stop his
shouting."

She raised her voice against the
closing door:

"Who wants to hear your news, you—
dreadful fool?"

The Fear

A LANTERN light from deeper in the
barn
Shone on a man and woman in the
door
And threw their lurching shadows on a
house
Near by, all dark in every glossy
window.
A horse's hoof pawed once the hollow
floor,
And the back of the gig they stood
beside
Moved in a little. The man grasped a
wheel,
The woman spoke out sharply, "Whoa,
stand still!"
"I saw it just as plain as a white plate,"
She said, "as the light on the
dashboard ran
Along the bushes at the roadside—a
man's face.
You must have seen it too."
"I didn't see it.
Are you sure——"
"Yes, I'm sure!"
"—it was a face?"
"Joel, I'll have to look. I can't go in,
I can't, and leave a thing like that
unsettled.

Doors locked and curtains drawn will
make no difference.

I always have felt strange when we
came home

To the dark house after so long an
absence,

And the key rattled loudly into place

Seemed to warn someone to be getting
out

At one door as we entered at another.

What if I'm right, and someone all the
time—

Don't hold my arm!"

"I say it's someone passing."

"You speak as if this were a travelled
road.

You forget where we are. What is
beyond

That he'd be going to or coming from

At such an hour of night, and on foot
too.

What was he standing still for in the
bushes?"

"It's not so very late—it's only dark.

There's more in it than you're inclined
to say.

Did he look like——?"

"He looked like anyone.

I'll never rest to-night unless I know.

Give me the lantern."

"You don't want the lantern."

She pushed past him and got it for herself.

"You're not to come," she said. "This is my business.

If the time's come to face it, I'm the one

To put it the right way. He'd never dare—

Listen! He kicked a stone. Hear that, hear that!

He's coming towards us. Joel, go in— please.

Hark!—I don't hear him now. But please go in."

"In the first place you can't make me believe it's——"

"It is—or someone else he's sent to watch.

And now's the time to have it out with him

While we know definitely where he is.

Let him get off and he'll be everywhere

Around us, looking out of trees and bushes

Till I sha'n't dare to set a foot outdoors.

And I can't stand it. Joel, let me go!"

"But it's nonsense to think he'd care enough."

"You mean you couldn't understand his caring.

Oh, but you see he hadn't had enough—

Joel, I won't—I won't—I promise you.

We mustn't say hard things. You mustn't either."

"I'll be the one, if anybody goes!

But you give him the advantage with this light.

What couldn't he do to us standing here!

And if to see was what he wanted, why

He has seen all there was to see and gone."

He appeared to forget to keep his hold,

But advanced with her as she crossed the grass.

"What do you want?" she cried to all the dark.

She stretched up tall to overlook the light

That hung in both hands hot against her skirt.

"There's no one; so you're wrong," he said.

"There is.—

What do you want?" she cried, and then herself

Was startled when an answer really came.

"Nothing." It came from well along the road.

She reached a hand to Joel for support:
The smell of scorching woollen made
her faint.

"What are you doing round this house
at night?"

"Nothing." A pause: there seemed no
more to say.

And then the voice again: "You seem
afraid.

I saw by the way you whipped up the
horse.

I'll just come forward in the lantern
light

And let you see."

"Yes, do.—Joel, go back!"

She stood her ground against the noisy
steps

That came on, but her body rocked a
little.

"You see," the voice said.

"Oh." She looked and looked.

"You don't see—I've a child here by
the hand."

"What's a child doing at this time of
night——?"

"Out walking. Every child should have
the memory

Of at least one long-after-bedtime
walk.

What, son?"

"Then I should think you'd try to find
Somewhere to walk——"

"The highway as it happens—

We're stopping for the fortnight down at Dean's."

"But if that's all—Joel—you realize—

You won't think anything. You understand?

You understand that we have to be careful.

This is a very, very lonely place.

Joel!" She spoke as if she couldn't turn.

The swinging lantern lengthened to the ground,

It touched, it struck it, clattered and went out.

The Self-seeker

"WILLIS, I didn't want you here to-day:

The lawyer's coming for the company.

I'm going to sell my soul, or, rather, feet.

Five hundred dollars for the pair, you know."

"With you the feet have nearly been the soul;

And if you're going to sell them to the devil,

I want to see you do it. When's he
coming?"

"I half suspect you knew, and came on
purpose

To try to help me drive a better
bargain."

"Well, if it's true! Yours are no
common feet.

The lawyer don't know what it is he's
buying:

So many miles you might have walked
you won't walk.

You haven't run your forty orchids
down.

What does he think?—How are the
blessed feet?

The doctor's sure you're going to walk
again?"

"He thinks I'll hobble. It's both legs
and feet."

"They must be terrible—I mean to
look at."

"I haven't dared to look at them
uncovered.

Through the bed blankets I remind
myself

Of a starfish laid out with rigid
points."

"The wonder is it hadn't been your
head."

"It's hard to tell you how I managed it.

When I saw the shaft had me by the coat,
　I didn't try too long to pull away,
　Or fumble for my knife to cut away,
　I just embraced the shaft and rode it out—
　Till Weiss shut off the water in the wheel-pit.
　That's how I think I didn't lose my head.
　But my legs got their knocks against the ceiling."
　"Awful. Why didn't they throw off the belt
　Instead of going clear down in the wheel-pit?"
　"They say some time was wasted on the belt—
　Old streak of leather—doesn't love me much
　Because I make him spit fire at my knuckles,
　The way Ben Franklin used to make the kite-string.
　That must be it. Some days he won't stay on.
　That day a woman couldn't coax him off.
　He's on his rounds now with his tail in his mouth
　Snatched right and left across the silver pulleys.

Everything goes the same without me
there.
You can hear the small buzz saws
whine, the big saw
Caterwaul to the hills around the
village
As they both bite the wood. It's all our
music.
One ought as a good villager to like it.
No doubt it has a sort of prosperous
sound,
And it's our life."
"Yes, when it's not our death."
"You make that sound as if it wasn't so
With everything. What we live by we
die by.
I wonder where my lawyer is. His
train's in.
I want this over with; I'm hot and
tired."
"You're getting ready to do something
foolish."
"Watch for him, will you, Will? You
let him in.
I'd rather Mrs. Corbin didn't know;
I've boarded here so long, she thinks
she owns me.
You're bad enough to manage without
her."
"And I'm going to be worse instead of
better.

You've got to tell me how far this is
gone:
   Have you agreed to any price?"
   "Five hundred.
   Five hundred—five—five! One, two,
three, four, five.
   You needn't look at me."
   "I don't believe you."
   "I told you, Willis, when you first
came in.
   Don't you be hard on me. I have to
take
   What I can get. You see they have the
feet,
   Which gives them the advantage in the
trade.
   I can't get back the feet in any case."
   "But your flowers, man, you're selling
out your flowers."
   "Yes, that's one way to put it—all the
flowers
   Of every kind everywhere in this
region
   For the next forty summers—call it
forty.
   But I'm not selling those, I'm giving
them,
   They never earned me so much as one
cent:
   Money can't pay me for the loss of
them.

No, the five hundred was the sum they named

To pay the doctor's bill and tide me over.

It's that or fight, and I don't want to fight—

I just want to get settled in my life,

Such as it's going to be, and know the worst,

Or best—it may not be so bad. The firm

Promise me all the shooks I want to nail."

"But what about your flora of the valley?"

"You have me there. But that—you didn't think

That was worth money to me? Still I own

It goes against me not to finish it

For the friends it might bring me. By the way,

I had a letter from Burroughs—did I tell you?—

About my Cyprepedium reginæ;

He says it's not reported so far north.

There! there's the bell. He's rung. But you go down

And bring him up, and don't let Mrs. Corbin.—

Oh, well, we'll soon be through with it. I'm tired."

Willis brought up besides the Boston lawyer

A little barefoot girl who in the noise

Of heavy footsteps in the old frame house,

And baritone importance of the lawyer,

Stood for a while unnoticed with her hands

Shyly behind her.

"Well, and how is Mister———"

The lawyer was already in his satchel

As if for papers that might bear the name

He hadn't at command. "You must excuse me,

I dropped in at the mill and was detained."

"Looking round, I suppose," said Willis.

"Yes,

Well, yes."

"Hear anything that might prove useful?"

The Broken One saw Anne. "Why, here is Anne.

What do you want, dear? Come, stand by the bed;

Tell me what is it?" Anne just wagged her dress

With both hands held behind her. "Guess," she said.

"Oh, guess which hand? My my! Once on a time
I knew a lovely way to tell for certain
By looking in the ears. But I forget it.
Er, let me see. I think I'll take the right.
That's sure to be right even if it's wrong.
Come, hold it out. Don't change.—A Ram's Horn orchid!
A Ram's Horn! What would I have got, I wonder,
If I had chosen left. Hold out the left.
Another Ram's Horn! Where did you find those,
Under what beech tree, on what woodchuck's knoll?"
Anne looked at the large lawyer at her side,
And thought she wouldn't venture on so much.
"Were there no others?"
"There were four or five.
I knew you wouldn't let me pick them all."
"I wouldn't—so I wouldn't. You're the girl!
You see Anne has her lesson learned by heart."
"I wanted there should be some there next year."

"Of course you did. You left the rest
for seed,

And for the backwoods woodchuck.
You're the girl!

A Ram's Horn orchid seedpod for a
woodchuck

Sounds something like. Better than
farmer's beans

To a discriminating appetite,

Though the Ram's Horn is seldom to
be had

In bushel lots—doesn't come on the
market.

But, Anne, I'm troubled; have you told
me all?

You're hiding something. That's as bad
as lying.

You ask this lawyer man. And it's not
safe

With a lawyer at hand to find you out.

Nothing is hidden from some people,
Anne.

You don't tell me that where you
found a Ram's Horn

You didn't find a Yellow Lady's
Slipper.

What did I tell you? What? I'd blush, I
would.

Don't you defend yourself. If it was
there,

Where is it now, the Yellow Lady's
Slipper?"

"Well, wait—it's common—it's too common."

"Common?

The Purple Lady's Slipper's commoner."

"I didn't bring a Purple Lady's Slipper

To You—to you I mean—they're both too common."

The lawyer gave a laugh among his papers

As if with some idea that she had scored.

"I've broken Anne of gathering bouquets.

It's not fair to the child. It can't be helped though:

Pressed into service means pressed out of shape.

Somehow I'll make it right with her— she'll see.

She's going to do my scouting in the field,

Over stone walls and all along a wood

And by a river bank for water flowers,

The floating Heart, with small leaf like a heart,

And at the sinus under water a fist

Of little fingers all kept down but one,

And that thrust up to blossom in the sun

As if to say, 'You! You're the Heart's desire.'

Anne has a way with flowers to take the place

Of that she's lost: she goes down on one knee

And lifts their faces by the chin to hers

And says their names, and leaves them where they are."

The lawyer wore a watch the case of which

Was cunningly devised to make a noise

Like a small pistol when he snapped it shut

At such a time as this. He snapped it now.

"Well, Anne, go, dearie. Our affair will wait.

The lawyer man is thinking of his train.

He wants to give me lots and lots of money

Before he goes, because I hurt myself,

And it may take him I don't know how long.

But put our flowers in water first. Will, help her:

The pitcher's too full for her. There's no cup?

Just hook them on the inside of the pitcher.

Now run.—Get out your documents! You see

I have to keep on the good side of
Anne.

I'm a great boy to think of number
one.

And you can't blame me in the place
I'm in.

Who will take care of my necessities
Unless I do?"

"A pretty interlude,"

The lawyer said. "I'm sorry, but my
train—

Luckily terms are all agreed upon.

You only have to sign your name.
Right—there."

"You, Will, stop making faces. Come
round here

Where you can't make them. What is it
you want?

I'll put you out with Anne. Be good or
go."

"You don't mean you will sign that
thing unread?"

"Make yourself useful then, and read it
for me.

Isn't it something I have seen before?"

"You'll find it is. Let your friend look
at it."

"Yes, but all that takes time, and I'm
as much

In haste to get it over with as you.

But read it, read it. That's right, draw
the curtain:

Half the time I don't know what's
troubling me.—

What do you say, Will? Don't you be a
fool,

You! crumpling folkses legal
documents.

Out with it if you've any real
objection."

"Five hundred dollars!"

"What would you think right?"

"A thousand wouldn't be a cent too
much;

You know it, Mr. Lawyer. The sin is
Accepting anything before he knows
Whether he's ever going to walk again.
It smells to me like a dishonest trick."

"I think—I think—from what I heard
to-day—

And saw myself—he would be ill-
advised——"

"What did you hear, for instance?"
Willis said.

"Now the place where the accident
occurred——"

The Broken One was twisted in his
bed.

"This is between you two apparently.

Where I come in is what I want to
know.

You stand up to it like a pair of cocks.

Go outdoors if you want to fight.
Spare me.

When you come back, I'll have the papers signed.

Will pencil do? Then, please, your fountain pen.

One of you hold my head up from the pillow."

Willis flung off the bed. "I wash my hands—

I'm no match—no, and don't pretend to be——"

The lawyer gravely capped his fountain pen.

"You're doing the wise thing: you won't regret it.

We're very sorry for you."

Willis sneered:

"Who's we?—some stockholders in Boston?

I'll go outdoors, by gad, and won't come back."

"Willis, bring Anne back with you when you come.

Yes. Thanks for caring. Don't mind Will: he's savage.

He thinks you ought to pay me for my flowers.

You don't know what I mean about the flowers.

Don't stop to try to now. You'll miss your train.

Good-bye." He flung his arms around his face.

The Wood-pile

OUT walking in the frozen swamp one grey day
I paused and said, "I will turn back from here.
No, I will go on farther—and we shall see."
The hard snow held me, save where now and then
One foot went down. The view was all in lines
Straight up and down of tall slim trees
Too much alike to mark or name a place by
So as to say for certain I was here
Or somewhere else: I was just far from home.
A small bird flew before me. He was careful
To put a tree between us when he lighted,
And say no word to tell me who he was
Who was so foolish as to think what he thought.
He thought that I was after him for a feather—

The white one in his tail; like one who takes

Everything said as personal to himself.

One flight out sideways would have undeceived him.

And then there was a pile of wood for which

I forgot him and let his little fear

Carry him off the way I might have gone,

Without so much as wishing him good-night.

He went behind it to make his last stand.

It was a cord of maple, cut and split

And piled—and measured, four by four by eight.

And not another like it could I see.

No runner tracks in this year's snow looped near it.

And it was older sure than this year's cutting,

Or even last year's or the year's before.

The wood was grey and the bark warping off it

And the pile somewhat sunken. Clematis

Had wound strings round and round it like a bundle.

What held it though on one side was a tree

Still growing, and on one a stake and prop,

These latter about to fall. I thought that only

Someone who lived in turning to fresh tasks

Could so forget his handiwork on which

He spent himself, the labour of his axe,

And leave it there far from a useful fireplace

To warm the frozen swamp as best it could

With the slow smokeless burning of decay.

Good Hours

I HAD for my winter evening walk—
No one at all with whom to talk,
But I had the cottages in a row
Up to their shining eyes in snow.
And I thought I had the folk within:
I had the sound of a violin;
I had a glimpse through curtain laces
Of youthful forms and youthful faces.
I had such company outward bound.

I went till there were no cottages
found.
I turned and repented, but coming
back
I saw no window but that was black.
Over the snow my creaking feet
Disturbed the slumbering village street
Like profanation, by your leave,
At ten o'clock of a winter eve.

CPSIA information can be obtained
at www.ICGtesting.com
Printed in the USA
BVHW031547130819
555787BV00001B/166/P